HAPPY DAYS

HAPPY DAYS

A play in two acts

SAMUEL BECKETT

faber and faber

LONDON · BOSTON

First published in the USA in 1961
by Grove Press Inc., New York
First published in Great Britain in 1963
by Faber and Faber Limited
3 Queen Square London WCIN 3AU
First published in Faber paperbacks 1966

Printed in England by Clays Ltd, St Ives plc
All rights reserved
© Grove Press Inc., 1961

All applications for performing rights
should be addressed to:
Curtis Brown Ltd 162/168 Regent Street
London WIR 5TA

A CIP record for this book
is available from the British Library

ISBN 0-571-06653-4

14 16 18 20 19 17 15

First performed in New York on 17 September 1961 at the
Cherry Lane Theatre.

WINNIE   Ruth White
WILLIE   John C. Becher

Director   Alan Schneider

CHARACTERS

WINNIE   *a woman of about fifty*
WILLIE   *a man of about sixty*

ACT ONE

*Expanse of scorched grass rising centre to low mound. Gentle
slopes down to front and either side of stage. Back an abrupter
fall to stage level. Maximum of simplicity and symmetry.*

   Blazing light.

   *Very pompier trompe-l'oeil backcloth to represent unbroken
plain and sky receding to meet in far distance.*

   Embedded up to above her waist in exact centre of mound,
WINNIE. *About fifty, well-preserved, blonde for preference,
plump, arms and shoulders bare, low bodice, big bosom, pearl
necklace. She is discovered sleeping, her arms on the ground
before her, her head on her arms. Beside her on ground to her
left a capacious black bag, shopping variety, and to her right a
collapsible collapsed parasol, beak of handle emerging from
sheath.*

   *To her right and rear, lying asleep on ground, hidden by
mound,* WILLIE.

   *Long pause. A bell rings piercingly, say ten seconds, stops.
She does not move. Pause. Bell more piercingly, say five
seconds. She wakes. Bell stops. She raises her head, gazes front.
Long pause. She straightens up, lays her hands flat on ground,
throws back her head and gazes at zenith. Long pause.*

WINNIE: [*Gazing at zenith.*] Another heavenly day. [*Pause.
   Head back level, eyes front, pause. She clasps hands to
   breast, closes eyes. Lips move in inaudible prayer, say ten
   seconds. Lips still. Hands remain clasped. Low.*] For Jesus
   Christ sake Amen. [*Eyes open, hands unclasp, return to
   mound. Pause. She clasps hands to breast again, closes
   eyes, lips move again in inaudible addendum, say five
   seconds. Low.*] World without end Amen. [*Eyes open,
   hands unclasp, return to mound. Pause.*] Begin, Winnie.
   [*Pause.*] Begin your day, Winnie. [*Pause. She turns to bag,
   rummages in it without moving it from its place, brings*

out toothbrush, rummages again, brings out flat tube of toothpaste, turns back front, unscrews cap of tube, lays cap on ground, squeezes with difficulty small blob of paste on brush, holds tube in one hand and brushes teeth with other. She turns modestly aside and back to her right to spit out behind mound. In this position her eyes rest on WILLIE. *She spits out. She cranes a little farther back and down. Loud.*] Hoo-oo! [*Pause. Louder.*] Hoo-oo! [*Pause. Tender smile as she turns back front, lays down brush.*] Poor Willie – [*examines tube, smile off*] – running out – [*looks for cap*] – ah well – [*finds cap*] – can't be helped – [*screws on cap*] – just one of those old things – [*lays down tube*] – another of those old things – [*turns towards bag*] – just can't be cured – [*rummages in bag*] – cannot be cured – [*brings out small mirror, turns back front*] – ah yes – [*inspects teeth in mirror*] – poor dear Willie – [*testing upper front teeth with thumb, indistinctly*] – good Lord! – [*pulling back upper lip to inspect gums, do.*] – good God! – [*pulling back corner of mouth, mouth open, do.*] – ah well – [*other corner, do.*] – no worse – [*abandons inspection, normal speech*] – no better, no worse – [*lays down mirror*] – no change – [*wipes fingers on grass*] – no pain – [*looks for toothbrush*] – hardly any – [*takes up toothbrush*] – great thing that – [*examines handle of brush*] – nothing like it – [*examines handle, reads*] – pure . . . what? – [*pause*] – what? – [*lays down brush*] – ah yes – [*turns towards bag*] – poor Willie – [*rummages in bag*] – no zest – [*rummages*] – for anything – [*brings out spectacles in case*] – no interest – [*turns back front*] – in life – [*takes spectacles from case*] – poor dear Willie – [*lays down case*] – sleep for ever – [*opens spectacles*] – marvellous gift – [*puts on spectacles*] – nothing to touch it – [*looks for toothbrush*] – in my opinion – [*takes up toothbrush*] – always said so – [*examines handle of brush*] – wish I had it – [*examines handle, reads*] – genuine . . . pure . . . what? – [*lays down brush*] – blind next – [*takes off spectacles*] – ah well – [*lays down spectacles*] – seen enough – [*feels in bodice for handkerchief*] – I suppose – [*takes out folded*

handkerchief] – by now – *[shakes out handkerchief]* –
what are those wonderful lines – *[wipes one eye]* – woe
woe is me – *[wipes the other]* – to see what I see – *[looks
for spectacles]* – ah yes – *[takes up spectacles]* – wouldn't
miss it – *[starts polishing spectacles, breathing on lenses]* –
or would I? – *[polishes]* – holy light – *[polishes]* – bob up
out of dark – *[polishes]* – blaze of hellish light. *[Stops
polishing, raises face to sky, pause, head back level,
resumes polishing, stops polishing, cranes back to her right
and down.]* Hoo-oo! *[Pause. Tender smile as she turns
back front and resumes polishing. Smile off.]* Marvellous
gift – *[stops polishing, lays down spectacles]* – wish I had
it – *[folds handkerchief]* – ah well – *[puts handkerchief
back in bodice]* – can't complain – *[looks for spectacles]* –
no no – *[takes up spectacles]* – mustn't complain – *[holds
up spectacles, looks through lens]* – so much to be
thankful for – *[looks through other lens]* – no pain – *[puts
on spectacles]* – hardly any – *[looks for toothbrush]* –
wonderful thing that – *[takes up toothbrush]* – nothing
like it – *[examines handle of brush]* – slight headache
sometimes – *[examines handle, reads]* – guaranteed . . .
genuine . . . pure . . . what? – *[looks closer]* – genuine
pure . . . – *[takes handkerchief from bodice]* – ah yes –
[shakes out handkerchief] – occasional mild migraine –
[starts wiping handle of brush] – it comes – *[wipes]* – then
goes – *[wiping mechanically]* – ah yes – *[wiping]* – many
mercies – *[wiping]* – great mercies – *[stops wiping, fixed
lost gaze, brokenly]* – prayers perhaps not for naught –
[pause, do.] – first thing – *[pause, do.]* – last thing – *[head
down, resumes wiping, stops wiping, head up, calmed,
wipes eyes, folds handkerchief, puts it back in bodice,
examines handle of brush, reads]* – fully guaranteed . . .
genuine pure . . . – *[looks closer]* – genuine pure . . .
*[Takes off spectacles, lays them and brush down, gazes
before her.]* Old things. *[Pause.]* Old eyes. *[Long pause.]*
On, Winnie. *[She casts about her, sees parasol, considers it
at length, takes it up and develops from sheath a handle of
surprising length. Holding butt of parasol in right hand she
cranes back and down to her right to hang over* WILLIE.]

Hoo-oo! [*Pause.*] Willie! [*Pause.*] Wonderful gift. [*She
strikes down at him with beak of parasol.*] Wish I had it.
[*She strikes again. The parasol slips from her grasp and
falls behind mound. It is immediately restored to her by*
WILLIE'*s invisible hand.*] Thank you, dear. [*She transfers
parasol to left hand, turns back front and examines right
palm.*] Damp. [*Returns parasol to right hand, examines
left palm.*] Ah well, no worse. [*Head up, cheerfully.*] No
better, no worse, no change. [*Pause. Do.*] No pain.
[*Cranes back to look down at* WILLIE, *holding parasol by
butt as before.*] Don't go off on me again now dear will
you please, I may need you. [*Pause.*] No hurry, no hurry,
just don't curl up on me again. [*Turns back front, lays
down parasol, examines palms together, wipes them on
grass.*] Perhaps a shade off colour just the same. [*Turns to
bag, rummages in it, brings out revolver, holds it up, kisses
it rapidly, puts it back, rummages, brings out almost
empty bottle of red medicine, turns back front, looks for
spectacles, puts them on, reads label.*] Loss of spirits . . .
lack of keenness . . . want of appetite . . . infants . . .
children . . . adults . . . six level . . . tablespoonfuls daily –
[*head up, smile*] – the old style! – [*smile off, head down,
reads*] – daily . . . before and after . . . meals . . .
instantaneous . . . [*looks closer*] . . . improvement. [*Takes
off spectacles, lays them down, holds up bottle at arm's
length to see level, unscrews cap, swigs it off head well
back, tosses cap and bottle away in* WILLIE'*s direction.
Sound of breaking glass.*] Ah that's better! [*Turns to bag,
rummages in it, brings out lipstick, turns back front,
examines lipstick.*] Running out. [*Looks for spectacles.*] Ah
well. [*Puts on spectacles, looks for mirror.*] Mustn't
complain. [*Takes up mirror, starts doing lips.*] What is that
wonderful line? [*Lips.*] Oh fleeting joys – [*lips*] – oh
something lasting woe. [*Lips. She is interrupted by
disturbance from* WILLIE. *He is sitting up. She lowers
lipstick and mirror and cranes back and down to look at
him. Pause. Top back of* WILLIE'*s bald head, trickling
blood, rises to view above slope, comes to rest.* WINNIE
pushes up her spectacles. Pause. His hand appears with*

handkerchief, spreads it on skull, disappears. Pause. The
hand appears with boater, club ribbon, settles it on head,
rakish angle, disappears. Pause. WINNIE *cranes a little*
further back and down.] Slip on your drawers, dear, before
you get singed. [*Pause.*] No? [*Pause.*] Oh I see, you still
have some of that stuff left. [*Pause.*] Work it well in, dear.
[*Pause.*] Now the other. [*Pause. She turns back front,*
gazes before her. Happy expression.] Oh this is going to be
another happy day! [*Pause. Happy expression off. She*
pulls down spectacles and resumes lips. WILLIE *opens*
newspaper, hands invisible. Tops of yellow sheets appear
on either side of his head. WINNIE *finishes lips, inspects*
them in mirror held a little further away.] Ensign crimson.
[WILLIE *turns page.* WINNIE *lays down lipstick and*
mirror, turns towards bag.] Pale flag.
[WILLIE *turns page.* WINNIE *rummages in bag, brings out*
small ornate brimless hat with crumpled feather, turns
back front, straightens hat, smooths feather, raises it
towards head, arrests gesture as WILLIE *reads.*]

WILLIE: His Grace and Most Reverend Father in God Dr
Carolus Hunter dead in tub.
[*Pause.*]

WINNIE: [*Gazing front, hat in hand, tone of fervent*
reminiscence.] Charlie Hunter! [*Pause.*] I close my eyes —
[*she takes off spectacles and does so, hat in one hand,*
spectacles in other, WILLIE *turns page*] — and am sitting
on his knees again, in the back garden at Borough Green,
under the horse-beech. [*Pause. She opens eyes, puts on*
spectacles, fiddles with hat.] Oh the happy memories!
[*Pause. She raises hat towards head, arrests gesture as*
WILLIE *reads.*]

WILLIE: Opening for smart youth.
[*Pause. She raises hat towards head, arrests gesture, takes*
off spectacles, gazes front, hat in one hand, spectacles in
other.]

WINNIE: My first ball! [*Long pause.*] My second ball! [*Long*
pause. Closes eyes.] My first kiss! [*Pause.* WILLIE *turns*
page. WINNIE *opens eyes.*] A Mr Johnson, or Johnston, or
perhaps I should say Johnstone. Very bushy moustache,

very tawny. [*Reverently.*] Almost ginger! [*Pause.*] Within a toolshed, though whose I cannot conceive. We had no toolshed and he most certainly had no toolshed. [*Closes eyes.*] I see the piles of pots. [*Pause.*] The tangles of bast. [*Pause.*] The shadows deepening among the rafters. [*Pause. She opens eyes, puts on spectacles, raises hat towards head, arrests gesture as* WILLIE *reads.*]

WILLIE: Wanted bright boy.

[*Pause.* WINNIE *puts on hat hurriedly, looks for mirror.* WILLIE *turns page.* WINNIE *takes up mirror, inspects hat, lays down mirror, turns towards bag. Paper disappears.* WINNIE *rummages in bag, brings out magnifying-glass, turns back front, looks for toothbrush. Paper reappears, folded, and begins to fan* WILLIE's *face, hand invisible.* WINNIE *takes up toothbrush and examines handle through glass.*]

WINNIE: Fully guaranteed . . . [WILLIE *stops fanning*] . . . genuine pure . . . [*Pause.* WILLIE *resumes fanning.* WINNIE *looks closer, reads.*] Fully guaranteed . . . [WILLIE *stops fanning*] . . . genuine pure . . . [*Pause.* WILLIE *resumes fanning.* WINNIE *lays down glass and brush, takes handkerchief from bodice, takes off and polishes spectacles, puts on spectacles, looks for glass, takes up and polishes glass, lays down glass, looks for brush, takes up brush and wipes handle, lays down brush, puts handkerchief back in bodice, looks for glass, takes up glass, looks for brush, takes up brush and examines handle through glass.*] Fully guaranteed . . . [WILLIE *stops fanning*] . . . genuine pure . . . [*pause,* WILLIE *resumes fanning*] . . . hog's . . . [WILLIE *stops fanning, pause*] . . . setae. [*Pause.* WINNIE *lays down glass and brush, paper disappears,* WINNIE *takes off spectacles, lays them down, gazes front.*] Hog's setae. [*Pause.*] That is what I find so wonderful, that not a day goes by – [*smile*] – to speak in the old style – [*smile off*] – hardly a day, without some addition to one's knowledge however trifling, the addition I mean, provided one takes the pains. [WILLIE's *hand reappears with a postcard which he examines close to eyes.*] And if for some strange reason no further pains

are possible, why then just close the eyes – [*she does so*] –
and wait for the day to come – [*opens eyes*] – the happy
day to come when flesh melts at so many degrees and the
night of the moon has so many hundred hours. [*Pause.*]
That is what I find so comforting when I lose heart and
envy the brute beast. [*Turning towards* WILLIE.] I hope
you are taking in – [*She sees postcard, bends lower.*] What
is that you have there, Willie, may I see? [*She reaches
down with hand and* WILLIE *hands her card. The hairy
forearm appears above slope, raised in gesture of giving,
the hand open to take back, and remains in this position
till card is returned.* WINNIE *turns back front and
examines card.*] Heavens what are they up to! [*She looks
for spectacles, puts them on and examines card.*] No but
this is just genuine pure filth! [*Examines card.*] Make any
nice-minded person want to vomit! [*Impatience of* WILLIE'S
*fingers. She looks for glass, takes it up and examines card
through glass. Long pause.*] What does that creature in the
background think he's doing? [*Looks closer.*] Oh no
really! [*Impatience of fingers. Last long look. She lays
down glass, takes edge of card between right forefinger
and thumb, averts head, takes nose between left forefinger
and thumb.*] Pah! [*Drops card.*] Take it away! [WILLIE'S
*arm disappears. His hand reappears immediately, holding
card.* WINNIE *takes off spectacles, lays them down, gazes
before her. During what follows* WILLIE *continues to
relish card, varying angles and distance from his eyes.*]
Hog's setae. [*Puzzled expression.*] What exactly is a hog?
[*Pause. Do.*] A sow of course I know, but a hog . . .
[*Puzzled expression off.*] Oh well what does it matter, that
is what I always say, it will come back, that is what I find
so wonderful, all comes back. [*Pause.*] All? [*Pause.*] No,
not all. [*Smile.*] No no. [*Smile off.*] Not quite. [*Pause.*] A
part. [*Pause.*] Floats up, one fine day, out of the blue.
[*Pause.*] That is what I find so wonderful. [*Pause. She
turns towards bag. Hand and card disappear. She makes to
rummage in bag, arrests gesture.*] No. [*She turns back
front. Smile.*] No no. [*Smile off.*] Gently Winnie. [*She gazes
front.* WILLIE'S *hand reappears, takes off hat, disappears*

with hat.] What then? [*Hand reappears, takes
handkerchief from skull, disappears with handkerchief.
Sharply, as to one not paying attention.*] Winnie! [WILLIE
bows head out of sight.] What *is* the alternative? [*Pause.*]
What *is* the al – [WILLIE *blows nose loud and long, head
and hands invisible. She turns to look at him. Pause. Head
reappears. Pause. Hand reappears with handkerchief,
spreads it on skull, disappears. Pause. Hand reappears
with boater, settles it on head, rakish angle, disappears.
Pause.*] Would I had let you sleep on. [*She turns back
front. Intermittent plucking at grass, head up and down, to
animate following.*] Ah yes, if only I could bear to be
alone, I mean prattle away with not a soul to hear.
[*Pause.*] Not that I flatter myself you hear much, no Willie,
God forbid. [*Pause.*] Days perhaps when you hear nothing.
[*Pause.*] But days too when you answer. [*Pause.*] So that I
may say at all times, even when you do not answer and
perhaps hear nothing, something of this is being heard, I
am not merely talking to myself, that is in the wilderness, a
thing I could never bear to do – for any length of time.
[*Pause.*] That is what enables me to go on, go on talking
that is. [*Pause.*] Whereas if you were to die – [*smile*] – to
speak in the old style – [*smile off*] – or go away and leave
me, then what would I do, what *could* I do, all day long, I
mean between the bell for waking and the bell for sleep?
[*Pause.*] Simply gaze before me with compressed lips.
[*Long pause while she does so. No more plucking.*] Not
another word as long as I drew breath, nothing to break
the silence of this place. [*Pause.*] Save possibly, now and
then, every now and then, a sigh into my looking-glass.
[*Pause.*] Or a brief . . . gale of laughter, should I happen to
see the old joke again. [*Pause. Smile appears, broadens and
seems about to culminate in laugh when suddenly replaced
by expression of anxiety.*] My hair! [*Pause.*] Did I brush
and comb my hair? [*Pause.*] I may have done. [*Pause.*]
Normally I do. [*Pause.*] There is so little one *can* do.
[*Pause.*] One does it all. [*Pause.*] All one can. [*Pause.*] 'Tis
only human. [*Pause.*] Human nature. [*She begins to
inspect mound, looks up.*] Human weakness. [*She resumes*

inspection of mound, looks up.] Natural weakness. [*She resumes inspection of mound.*] I see no comb. [*Inspects.*] Nor any hairbrush. [*Looks up. Puzzled expression. She turns to bag, rummages in it.*] The comb is here. [*Back front. Puzzled expression. Back to bag. Rummages.*] The brush is here. [*Back front. Puzzled expression.*] Perhaps I put them back, after use. [*Pause. Do.*] But normally I do not put things back, after use, no, I leave them lying about and put them back all together, at the end of the day. [*Smile.*] To speak in the old style. [*Pause.*] The sweet old style. [*Smile off.*] And yet . . . I seem . . . to remember . . . [*Suddenly careless.*] Oh well, what does it matter, that is what I always say, I shall simply brush and comb them later on, purely and simply, I have the whole — [*Pause. Puzzled.*] Them? [*Pause.*] Or it? [*Pause.*] Brush and comb it? [*Pause.*] Sounds improper somehow. [*Pause. Turning a little towards* WILLIE.] What would you say, Willie? [*Pause. Turning a little further.*] What would you say, Willie, speaking of your hair, them or it? [*Pause.*] The hair on your head, I mean. [*Pause. Turning a little further.*] The hair on your head, Willie, what would you say speaking of the hair on your head, them or it? [*Long pause.*]

WILLIE: It.

WINNIE: [*Turning back front, joyful.*] Oh you are going to talk to me today, this is going to be a happy day! [*Pause. Joy off.*] Another happy day. [*Pause.*] Ah well, where was I, my hair, yes, later on, I shall be thankful for it later on. [*Pause.*] I have my — [*raises hands to hat*] — yes, on, my hat on — [*lowers hands*] — I cannot take it off now. [*Pause.*] To think there are times one cannot take off one's hat, not if one's life were at stake. Times one cannot put it on, times one cannot take it off. [*Pause.*] How often I have said, Put on your hat now, Winnie, there is nothing else for it, take off your hat now, Winnie, like a good girl, it will do you good, and did not. [*Pause.*] Could not. [*Pause. She raises hand, frees a strand of hair from under hat, draws it towards eye, squints at it, lets it go, hand down.*] Golden you called it, that day, when the last guest was gone — [*hand up in gesture of raising a glass*] — to your golden . . .

may it never . . . [*voice breaks*] . . . may it never . . . [*Hand down. Head down. Pause. Low.*] That day. [*Pause. Do.*] What day? [*Pause. Head up. Normal voice.*] What now? [*Pause.*] Words fail, there are times when even they fail. [*Turning a little towards* WILLIE.] Is that not so, Willie? [*Pause. Turning a little further.*] Is not that so, Willie, that even words fail, at times? [*Pause. Back front.*] What is one to do then, until they come again? Brush and comb the hair, if it has not been done, or if there is some doubt, trim the nails if they are in need of trimming, these things tide one over. [*Pause.*] That is what I mean. [*Pause.*] That is all I mean. [*Pause.*] That is what I find so wonderful, that not a day goes by — [*smile*] — to speak in the old style — [*smile off*] — without some blessing — [WILLIE *collapses behind slope, his head disappears,* WINNIE *turns towards event*] — in disguise. [*She cranes back and down.*] Go back into your hole now, Willie, you've exposed yourself enough. [*Pause.*] Do as I say, Willie, don't lie sprawling there in this hellish sun, go back into your hole. [*Pause.*] Go on now, Willie. [WILLIE *invisible starts crawling left towards hole.*] That's the man. [*She follows his progress with her eyes.*] Not head first, stupid, how are you going to turn? [*Pause.*] That's it . . . right round . . . now . . . back in. [*Pause.*] Oh I know it is not easy, dear, crawling backwards, but it is rewarding in the end. [*Pause.*] You have left your vaseline behind. [*She watches as he crawls back for vaseline.*] The lid! [*She watches as he crawls back towards hole. Irritated.*] Not head first, I tell you! [*Pause.*] More to the right. [*Pause.*] The *right*, I said. [*Pause. Irritated.*] Keep your tail down, can't you! [*Pause.*] Now. [*Pause.*] There! [*All these directions loud. Now in her normal voice, still turned towards him.*] Can you hear me? [*Pause.*] I beseech you, Willie, just yes or no, can you hear me, just yes or nothing.
[*Pause.*]

WILLIE: Yes.

WINNIE: [*Turning front, same voice.*] And now?

WILLIE: [*Irritated.*] Yes.

WINNIE: [*Less loud.*] And now?

WILLIE: [*More irritated.*] Yes.

WINNIE: [*Still less loud.*] And now? [*A little louder.*] And now?

WILLIE: [*Violently.*] Yes!

WINNIE: [*Same voice.*] Fear no more the heat o' the sun.
[*Pause.*] Did you hear that?

WILLIE: [*Irritated.*] Yes.

WINNIE: [*Same voice.*] What? [*Pause.*] What?

WILLIE: [*More irritated.*] Fear no more.
[*Pause.*]

WINNIE: [*Same voice.*] No more what? [*Pause.*] Fear no more
what?

WILLIE: [*Violently.*] Fear no more!

WINNIE: [*Normal voice, gabbled.*] Bless you Willie I do
appreciate your goodness I know what an effort it costs
you, now you may relax I shall not trouble you again
unless I am obliged to, by that I mean unless I come to the
end of my own resources which is most unlikely, just to
know that in theory you can hear me even though in fact
you don't is all I need, just to feel you there within earshot
and conceivably on the qui vive is all I ask, not to say
anything I would not wish you to hear or liable to cause
you pain, not to be just babbling away on trust as it is
were not knowing and something gnawing at me. [*Pause
for breath.*] Doubt. [*Places index and second finger on
heart area, moves them about, brings them to rest.*] Here.
[*Moves them slightly.*] Abouts. [*Hand away.*] Oh no doubt
the time will come when before I can utter a word I must
make sure you heard the one that went before and then no
doubt another come another time when I must learn to
talk to myself a thing I could never bear to do such
wilderness. [*Pause.*] Or gaze before me with compressed
lips. [*She does so.*] All day long. [*Gaze and lips again.*] No.
[*Smile.*] No no. [*Smile off.*] There is of course the bag.
[*Turns towards it.*] There will always be the bag. [*Back
front.*] Yes, I suppose so. [*Pause.*] Even when you are gone,
Willie. [*She turns a little towards him.*] You *are* going,
Willie, aren't you? [*Pause. Louder.*] You *will* be going
soon, Willie, won't you? [*Pause. Louder.*] Willie! [*Pause.
She cranes back and down to look at him.*] So you have

taken off your straw, that is wise. [*Pause.*] You do look
snug, I must say, with your chin on your hands and the old
blue eyes like saucers in the shadows. [*Pause.*] Can you see
me from there I wonder, I still wonder. [*Pause.*] No? [*Back
front.*] Oh I know it does not follow when two are
gathered together – [*faltering*] – in this way – [*normal*] –
that because one sees the other the other sees the one, life
has taught me that . . . too. [*Pause.*] Yes, life I suppose,
there is no other word. [*She turns a little towards him.*]
Could you see me, Willie, do you think, from where you
are, if you were to raise your eyes in my direction? [*Turns
a little further.*] Lift up your eyes to me, Willie, and tell me
can you see me, do that for me, I'll lean back as far as I
can. [*Does so. Pause.*] No? [*Pause.*] Well never mind.
[*Turns back painfully front.*] The earth is very tight today,
can it be I have put on flesh, I trust not. [*Pause. Absently,
eyes lowered.*] The great heat possibly. [*Starts to pat and
stroke ground.*] All things expanding, some more than
others. [*Pause. Patting and stroking.*] Some less. [*Pause.
Do.*] Oh I can well imagine what is passing through your
mind, it is not enough to have to listen to the woman, now
I must look at her as well. [*Pause. Do.*] Well it is very
understandable. [*Pause. Do.*] Most understandable.
[*Pause. Do.*] One does not appear to be asking a great
deal, indeed at times it would seem hardly possible –
[*voice breaks, falls to a murmur*] – to ask less – of a
fellow-creature – to put it mildly – whereas actually –
when you think about it – look into your heart – see the
other – what he needs – peace – to be left in peace – then
perhaps the moon – all this time – asking for the moon.
[*Pause. Stroking hand suddenly still. Lively.*] Oh I say,
what have we here? [*Bending head to ground,
incredulous.*] Looks like life of some kind! [*Looks for
spectacles, puts them on, bends closer. Pause.*] An emmet!
[*Recoils. Shrill.*] Willie, an emmet, a live emmet! [*Seizes
magnifying-glass, bends to ground again, inspects through
glass.*] Where's it gone? [*Inspects.*] Ah! [*Follows its
progress through grass.*] Has like a little white ball in its
arms. [*Follows progress. Hand still. Pause.*] It's gone in.

[*Continues a moment to gaze at spot through glass, then slowly straightens up, lays down glass, takes off spectacles and gazes before her, spectacles in hand. Finally.*] Like a little white ball. [*Long pause. Gesture to lay down spectacles.*]

WILLIE: Eggs.

WINNIE: [*Arresting gesture.*) What?
[*Pause.*]

WILLIE: Eggs. [*Pause. Gesture to lay down glasses.*] Formication.

WINNIE: [*Arresting gesture.*] What?
[*Pause.*]

WILLIE: Formication.
[*Pause. She lays down spectacles, gazes before her. Finally.*]

WINNIE: [*Murmur.*] God. [*Pause.* WILLIE *laughs quietly. After a moment she joins in. They laugh quietly together.* WILLIE *stops. She laughs on a moment alone.* WILLIE *joins in. They laugh together. She stops.* WILLIE *laughs on a moment alone. He stops. Pause. Normal voice.*] Ah well what a joy in any case to hear you laugh again, Willie, I was convinced I never would, you never would. [*Pause.*] I suppose some people might think us a trifle irreverent, but I doubt it. [*Pause.*] How can one better magnify the Almighty than by sniggering with him at his little jokes, particularly the poorer ones? [*Pause.*] I think you would back me up there, Willie. [*Pause.*] Or were we perhaps diverted by two quite different things? [*Pause.*] Oh well, what does it matter, that is what I always say, so long as one . . . you know . . . what is that wonderful line . . . laughing wild . . . something something laughing wild amid severest woe. [*Pause.*] And now? [*Long pause.*] Was I lovable once, Willie? [*Pause.*] Was I ever lovable? [*Pause.*] Do not misunderstand my question, I am not asking you if you loved me, we know all about that, I am asking you if you found me lovable – at one stage. [*Pause.*] No? [*Pause.*] You can't? [*Pause.*] Well I admit it is a teaser. And you have done more than your bit already, for the time being, just lie back now and relax, I shall not trouble you again unless I am compelled to, just to know you are there

within hearing and conceivably on the semi-alert is . . .
er . . . paradise enow. [*Pause.*] The day is now well
advanced. [*Smile.*] To speak in the old style. [*Smile off.*]
And yet it is perhaps a little soon for my song. [*Pause.*] To
sing too soon is a great mistake, I find. [*Turning towards
bag.*] There is of course the bag. [*Looking at bag.*] The bag.
[*Back front.*] Could I enumerate its contents? [*Pause.*] No.
[*Pause.*] Could I, if some kind person were to come along
and ask, What all have you got in that big black bag,
Winnie? give an exhaustive answer? [*Pause.*] No. [*Pause.*]
The depths in particular, who knows what treasures.
[*Pause.*] What comforts. [*Turns to look at bag.*] Yes, there is
the bag. [*Back front.*] But something tells me, Do not
overdo the bag, Winnie, make use of it of course, let it help
you . . . along, when stuck, by all means, but cast your mind
forward, something tells me, cast your mind forward,
Winnie, to the time when words must fail – [*she closes eyes,
pause, opens eyes*] – and do not overdo the bag. [*Pause. She
turns to look at bag.*] Perhaps just one quick dip. [*She turns
back front, closes eyes, throws out left arm, plunges hand in
bag and brings out revolver. Disgusted.*] You again! [*She
opens eyes, brings revolver front and contemplates it. She
weighs it in her palm.*] You'd think the weight of this thing
would bring it down among the . . . last rounds. But no. It
doesn't. Ever uppermost, like Browning. [*Pause.*]
Brownie . . . [*Turning a little towards* WILLIE.] Remember
Brownie, Willie? [*Pause.*] Remember how you used to keep
on at me to take it away from you? Take it away, Winnie,
take it away, before I put myself out of my misery. [*Back
front. Derisive.*] *Your* misery! [*To revolver.*] Oh I suppose
it's a comfort to know you're there, but I'm tired of you.
[*Pause.*] I'll leave you out, that's what I'll do. [*She lays
revolver on ground to her right.*] There, that's your home
from this day out. [*Smile.*] The old style! [*Smile off.*] And
now? [*Long pause.*] Is gravity what it was, Willie, I fancy
not. [*Pause.*] Yes, the feeling more and more that if I were
not held – [*gesture*] – in this way, I would simply float up
into the blue. [*Pause.*] And that perhaps some day the
earth will yield and let me go, the pull is so great, yes,

crack all round me and let me out. [*Pause.*] Don't you ever
have that feeling, Willie, of being sucked up? [*Pause.*]
Don't you have to cling on sometimes, Willie? [*Pause. She
turns a little towards him.*] Willie.
[*Pause.*]

WILLIE: *Sucked* up?

WINNIE: Yes love, up into the blue, like gossamer. [*Pause.*]
No? [*Pause.*] You don't? [*Pause.*] Ah well, natural laws,
natural laws, I suppose it's like everything else, it all
depends on the creature you happen to be. All I can say is
for my part is that for me they are not what they were
when I was young and . . . foolish and . . . [*faltering, head
down*] . . . beautiful . . . possibly . . . lovely . . . in a
way . . . to look at. [*Pause. Head up.*] Forgive me, Willie,
sorrow keeps breaking in. [*Normal voice.*] Ah well what a
joy in any case to know you are there, as usual, and
perhaps awake, and perhaps taking all this in, some of all
this, what a happy day for me . . . it will have been.
[*Pause.*] So far. [*Pause.*] What a blessing nothing grows,
imagine if all this stuff were to start growing. [*Pause.*]
Imagine. [*Pause.*] Ah yes, great mercies. [*Long pause.*] I
can say no more. [*Pause.*] For the moment. [*Pause. Turns
to look at bag. Back front. Smile.*] No no. [*Smile off.
Looks at parasol.*] I suppose I might – [*takes up parasol*] –
yes, I suppose I might . . . hoist this thing now. [*Begins to
unfurl it. Following punctuated by mechanical difficulties
overcome.*] One keeps putting off – putting up – for fear
of putting up too soon – and the day goes by – quite by –
without one's having put up – at all. [*Parasol now fully
open. Turned to her right she twirls it idly this way and
that.*] Ah yes, so little to say, so little to do, and the fear so
great, certain days, of finding oneself . . . left, with hours
still to run, before the bell for sleep, and nothing more to
say, nothing more to do, that the days go by, certain days
go by, quite by, the bell goes, and little or nothing said,
little or nothing done. [*Raising parasol.*] That is the
danger. [*Turning front.*] To be guarded against. [*She gazes
front, holding up parasol with right hand. Maximum
pause.*] I used to perspire freely. [*Pause.*] Now hardly at

all. [*Pause.*] The heat is much greater. [*Pause.*] The
perspiration much less. [*Pause.*] That is what I find so
wonderful. [*Pause.*] The way man adapts himself. [*Pause.*]
To changing conditions. [*She transfers parasol to left hand.
Long pause.*] Holding up wearies the arm. [*Pause.*] Not if
one is going along. [*Pause.*] Only if one is at rest. [*Pause.*]
That is a curious observation. [*Pause.*] I hope you heard
that, Willie, I should be grieved to think you had not heard
that. [*She takes parasol in both hands. Long pause.*] I am
weary, holding it up, and I cannot put it down. [*Pause.*] I
am worse off with it up than with it down, and I cannot
put it down. [*Pause.*] Reason says, Put it down, Winnie, it
is not helping you, put the thing down and get on with
something else. [*Pause.*] I cannot. [*Pause.*] I cannot move.
[*Pause.*] No, something must happen, in the world, take
place, some change, I cannot, if I am to move again.
[*Pause.*] Willie. [*Mildly.*] Help. [*Pause.*] No? [*Pause.*] Bid
me put this thing down, Willie, I would obey you instantly,
as I have always done, honoured and obeyed. [*Pause.*]
Please, Willie. [*Mildly.*] For pity's sake. [*Pause.*] No?
[*Pause.*] You can't? [*Pause.*]. Well I don't blame you, no, it
would ill become me, who cannot move, to blame my
Willie because he cannot speak. [*Pause.*] Fortunately I am
in tongue again. [*Pause.*] That is what I find so wonderful,
my two lamps, when one goes out the other burns
brighter. [*Pause.*] Oh yes, great mercies. [*Maximum pause.
The parasol goes on fire. Smoke, flames if feasible. She
sniffs, looks up, throws parasol to her right behind mound,
cranes back to watch it burning. Pause.*] Ah earth you old
extinguisher. [*Back front.*] I presume this has occurred
before, though I cannot recall it. [*Pause.*] Can you, Willie?
[*Turns a little towards him.*] Can you recall this having
occurred before? [*Pause. Cranes back to look at him.*] Do
you know what has occurred, Willie? [*Pause.*] Have you
gone off on me again? [*Pause.*] I do not ask if you are alive
to all that is going on, I merely ask if you have not gone
off on me again. [*Pause.*] Your eyes appear to be closed,
but that has no particular significance we know. [*Pause.*]
Raise a finger, dear, will you please, if you are not quite

senseless. [*Pause.*] Do that for me, Willie please, just the little finger, if you are still conscious. [*Pause. Joyful.*] Oh all five, you are a darling today, now I may continue with an easy mind. [*Back front.*] Yes, what ever occurred that did not occur before and yet . . . I wonder, yes, I confess I wonder. [*Pause.*] With the sun blazing so much fiercer down, and hourly fiercer, is it not natural things should go on fire never known to do so, in this way I mean, spontaneous like. [*Pause.*] Shall I myself not melt perhaps in the end, or burn, oh I do not mean necessarily burst into flames, no, just little by little be charred to a black cinder, all this – [*ample gesture of arms*] – visible flesh. [*Pause.*] On the other hand, did I ever know a temperate time? [*Pause.*] No. [*Pause.*] I speak of temperate times and torrid times, they are empty words. [*Pause.*] I speak of when I was not yet caught – in this way – and had my legs and had the use of my legs, and could seek out a shady place, like you, when I was tired of the sun, or a sunny place when I was tired of the shade, like you, and they are all empty words. [*Pause.*] It is no hotter today than yesterday, it will be no hotter tomorrow than today, how could it, and so on back into the far past, forward into the far future. [*Pause.*] And should one day the earth cover my breasts, then I shall never have seen my breasts, no one ever seen my breasts. [*Pause.*] I hope you caught something of that, Willie, I should be sorry to think you had caught nothing of all that, it is not every day I rise to such heights. [*Pause.*] Yes, something seems to have occurred, something has seemed to occur, and nothing has occurred, nothing at all, you are quite right, Willie. [*Pause.*] The sunshade will be there again tomorrow, beside me on this mound, to help me through the day. [*Pause. She takes up mirror.*] I take up this little glass, I shiver it on a stone – [*does so*] – I throw it away – [*does so far behind her*] – it will be in the bag again tomorrow, without a scratch, to help me through the day. [*Pause.*] No, one can do nothing. [*Pause.*] That is what I find so wonderful, the way things . . . [*voice breaks, head down*] . . . things . . . so wonderful. [*Long pause, head down. Finally turns, still bowed, to bag, brings*

*out unidentifiable odds and ends, stuffs them back,
fumbles deeper, brings out finally musical-box, winds it
up, turns it on, listens for a moment holding it in both
hands, huddled over it, turns back front, straightens up
and listens to tune, holding box to breast with both hands.
It plays the Waltz Duet 'I love you so' from The Merry
Widow. Gradually happy expression. She sways to the
rhythm. Music stops. Pause. Brief burst of hoarse song
without words – musical-box tune – from* WILLIE.
Increase of happy expression. She lays down box.] Oh this
will have been a happy day! [*She claps hands.*] Again,
Willie, again! [*Claps.*] Encore, Willie, please! [*Pause.
Happy expression off.*] No? You won't do that for me?
[*Pause.*] Well it is very understandable, very
understandable. One cannot sing just to please someone,
however much one loves them, no, song must come from
the heart, that is what I always say, pour out from the
inmost, like a thrush. [*Pause.*] How often I have said, in
evil hours, Sing now, Winnie, sing your song, there is
nothing else for it, and did not. [*Pause.*] Could not.
[*Pause.*] No, like the thrush, or the bird of dawning, with
no thought of benefit, to oneself or anyone else. [*Pause.*]
And now? [*Long pause. Low.*] Strange feeling. [*Pause.
Do.*] Strange feeling that someone is looking at me. I am
clear, then dim, then gone, then dim again, then clear
again, and so on, back and forth, in and out of someone's
eye. [*Pause. Do.*] Strange? [*Pause. Do.*] No, here all is
strange. [*Pause. Normal voice.*] Something says, Stop
talking now, Winnie, for a minute, don't squander all your
words for the day, stop talking and do something for a
change, will you? [*She raises hands and holds them open
before her eyes. Apostrophic.*] Do something! [*She closes
hands.*] What claws! [*She turns to bag, rummages in it,
brings out finally a nailfile, turns back front and begins to
file nails. Files for a time in silence, then the following
punctuated by filing.*] There floats up – into my thoughts –
a Mr Shower – a Mr and perhaps a Mrs Shower – no –
they are holding hands – his fiancée then more likely – or
just some – loved one. [*Looks closer at nails.*] Very brittle

today. [*Resumes filing.*] Shower – Shower – does the name mean anything – to you, Willie – evoke any reality, I mean – for you, Willie – don't answer if you don't – feel up to it – you have done more – than your bit – already – Shower – Shower. [*Inspects filed nails.*] Bit more like it. [*Raises head, gazes front.*] Keep yourself nice, Winnie, that's what I always say, come what may, keep yourself nice. [*Pause. Resumes filing.*] Yes – Shower – Shower – [*stops filing, raises head, gazes front, pause*] – or Cooker, perhaps I should say Cooker. [*Turning a little towards* WILLIE.] Cooker, Willie, does Cooker strike a chord? [*Pause. Turns a little further. Louder.*] Cooker, Willie, does Cooker ring a bell, the name Cooker? [*Pause. She cranes back to look at him. Pause.*] Oh really! [*Pause.*] Have you no handkerchief, darling? [*Pause.*] Have you no delicacy? [*Pause.*] Oh, Willie, you're not eating it! Spit it out, dear, spit it out! [*Pause. Back front.*] Ah well, I suppose it's only natural. [*Break in voice.*] Human. [*Pause. Do.*] What *is* one to do? [*Head down. Do.*] All day long. [*Pause. Do.*] Day after day. [*Pause. Head up. Smile. Calm.*] The old style! [*Smile off. Resumes nails.*] No, done him. [*Passes on to next.*] Should have put on my glasses. [*Pause.*] Too late now. [*Finishes left hand, inspects it.*] Bit more human. [*Starts right hand. Following punctuated as before.*] Well anyway – this man Shower – or Cooker – no matter – and the woman – hand in hand – in the other hands bags – kind of big brown grips – standing there gaping at me – and at last this man Shower – or Cooker – ends in 'er anyway – stake my life on that – What's she doing? he says – What's the idea? he says – stuck up to her diddies in the bleeding ground – coarse fellow – What does it mean? he says – What's it meant to mean? – and so on – lot more stuff like that – usual drivel – Do you hear me? he says – I do, she says, God help me – What do you mean, he says, God help you? [*Stops filing, raises head, gazes front.*] And you, she says, what's the idea of you, she says, what are you meant to mean? Is it because you're still on your two flat feet, with your old ditty full of tinned muck and changes of underwear, dragging me up and

down this fornicating wilderness, coarse creature, fit mate
– [*with sudden violence*] – let go of my hand and drop for
God's sake, she says, drop! [*Pause. Resumes filing.*] Why
doesn't he dig her out? he says – referring to you, my dear
– What good is she to him like that? – What good is he to
her like that? – and so on – usual tosh – Good! she says,
have a heart for God's sake – Dig her out, he says, dig her
out, no sense in her like that – Dig her out with what? she
says – I'd dig her out with my bare hands, he says – must
have been man and – wife. [*Files in silence.*] Next thing
they're away – hand in hand – and the bags – dim – then
gone – last human kind – to stray this way. [*Finishes right
hand, inspects it, lays down file, gazes front.*] Strange
thing, time like this, drift up into the mind. [*Pause.*]
Strange? [*Pause.*] No, here all is strange. [*Pause.*] Thankful
for it in any case. [*Voice breaks.*] Most thankful. [*Head
down. Pause. Head up. Calm.*] Bow and raise the head,
bow and raise, always that. [*Pause.*] And now? [*Long
pause. Starts putting things back in bag, toothbrush last.
This operation, interrupted by pauses as indicated,
punctuates following.*] It is perhaps a little soon – to make
ready – for the night – [*stops tidying, head up, smile*] –
the old style! – [*smile off, resumes tidying*] – and yet I do
– make ready for the night – feeling it at hand – the bell
for sleep – saying to myself – Winnie – it will not be long
now, Winnie – until the bell for sleep. [*Stops tidying, head
up.*] Sometimes I am wrong. [*Smile.*] But not often. [*Smile
off.*] Sometimes all is over, for the day, all done, all said,
all ready for the night, and the day not over, far from over,
the night not ready, far, far from ready. [*Smile.*] But not
often. [*Smile off.*] Yes, the bell for sleep, when I feel it at
hand, and so make ready for the night – [*gesture*] – in this
way, sometimes I am wrong – [*smile*] – but not often.
[*Smile off. Resumes tidying.*] I used to think – I say I used
to think – that all these things – put back into the bag – if
too soon – put back too soon – could be taken out again
– if necessary – if needed – and so on – indefinitely –
back into the bag – back out of the bag – until the bell –
went. [*Stops tidying, head up, smile.*] But no. [*Smile

broader.] No no. [*Smile off. Resumes tidying.*] I suppose
this — might seem strange — this — what shall I say — this
what I have said — yes — [*she takes up revolver*] — strange
— [*she turns to put revolver in bag*] — were it not — [*about
to put revolver in bag she arrests gesture and turns back
front*] — were it not — [*she lays down revolver to her right,
stops tidying, head up*] — that all seems strange. [*Pause.*]
Most strange. [*Pause.*] Never any change. [*Pause.*] And
more and more strange [*Pause. She bends to mound again,
takes up last object, i.e. toothbrush, and turns to put it in
bag when her attention is drawn to disturbance from
WILLIE. She cranes back and to her right to see. Pause.*]
Weary of your hole, dear? [*Pause.*] Well I can understand
that. [*Pause.*] Don't forget your straw. [*Pause.*] Not the
crawler you were, poor darling. [*Pause.*] No, not the
crawler I gave my heart to. [*Pause.*] The hands and knees,
love, try the hands and knees. [*Pause.*] The knees! The
knees! [*Pause.*] What a curse, mobility! [*She follows with
eyes his progress towards her behind mound, i.e. towards
place he occupied at beginning of act.*] Another foot,
Willie, and you're home. [*Pause as she observes last foot.*]
Ah! [*Turns back front laboriously, rubs neck.*] Crick in my
neck admiring you. [*Rubs neck.*] But it's worth it, well
worth it. [*Turning slightly towards him.*] Do you know
what I dream sometimes? [*Pause.*] What I dream
sometimes, Willie. [*Pause.*] That you'll come round and
live this side where I could see you. [*Pause. Back front.*] I'd
be a different woman. [*Pause.*] Unrecognizable. [*Turning
slightly towards him.*] Or just now and then, come round
this side just every now and then and let me feast on you.
[*Back front.*] But you can't, I know. [*Head down.*] I know.
[*Pause. Head up.*] Well anyway — [*looks at toothbrush in
her hand*] — can't be long now — [*looks at brush*] — until
the bell. [*Top back of WILLIE's head appears above slope.
WINNIE looks closer at brush.*] Fully guaranteed . . . [*head
up*] . . . what's this it was? [WILLIE's *hand appears with
handkerchief, spreads it on skull, disappears.*] Genuine
pure . . . fully guaranteed . . . [WILLIE's *hand appears with
boater, settles it on head, rakish angle, disappears*]

. . . genuine pure . . . ah! hog's setae. [*Pause.*] What is a hog exactly? [*Pause. Turns slightly towards* WILLIE.] What exactly is a hog, Willie, do you know, I can't remember. [*Pause. Turning a little further, pleading.*] What *is* a hog, Willie, please! [*Pause.*]

WILLIE: Castrated male swine. [*Happy expression appears on* WINNIE'*s face.*] Reared for slaughter. [*Happy expression increases.* WILLIE *opens newspaper, hands invisible. Tops of yellow sheets appear on either side of his head.* WINNIE *gazes before her with happy expression.*]

WINNIE: Oh this *is* a happy day! This will have been another happy day! [*Pause.*] After all. [*Pause.*] So far.
[*Pause. Happy expression off.* WILLIE *turns page. Pause. He turns another page. Pause.*]

WILLIE: Opening for smart youth.
[*Pause.* WINNIE *takes off hat, turns to put it in bag, arrests gesture, turns back front. Smile.*]

WINNIE: No. [*Smile broader.*] No no. [*Smile off. Puts on hat again, gazes front, pause.*] And now? [*Pause.*] Sing. [*Pause.*] Sing your song, Winnie. [*Pause.*] No? [*Pause.*] Then pray. [*Pause.*] Pray your prayer, Winnie.
[*Pause.* WILLIE *turns page. Pause.*]

WILLIE: Wanted bright boy.
[*Pause.* WILLIE *gazes before her.* WILLIE *turns page. Pause. Newspaper disappears. Long pause.*]

WINNIE: Pray your old prayer, Winnie.
[*Long pause.*]

CURTAIN

ACT TWO

Scene as before.

   WINNIE *embedded up to neck, hat on head, eyes closed. Her head, which she can no longer turn, nor bow, nor raise, faces front motionless throughout act. Movements of eyes as indicated.*

   Bag and parasol as before. Revolver conspicuous to her right on mound.

   Long pause.

   Bell rings loudly. She opens eyes at once. Bell stops. She gazes front. Long pause.

WINNIE: Hail, holy light. [*Long pause. She closes her eyes. Bell rings loudly. She opens eyes at once. Bell stops. She gazes front. Long smile. Smile off. Long pause.*] Someone is looking at me still. [*Pause.*] Caring for me still. [*Pause.*] That is what I find so wonderful. [*Pause.*] Eyes on my eyes. [*Pause.*] What is that unforgettable line? [*Pause. Eyes right.*] Willie. [*Pause. Louder.*] Willie. [*Pause. Eyes front.*] May one still speak of time? [*Pause.*] Say it is a long time now, Willie, since I saw you. [*Pause.*] Since I heard you. [*Pause.*] May one? [*Pause.*] One does. [*Smile.*] The old style! [*Smile off.*] There is so little one can speak of. [*Pause.*] One speaks of it all. [*Pause.*] All one can. [*Pause.*] I used to think . . . [*pause*] . . . I say I used to think that I would learn to talk alone. [*Pause.*] By that I mean to myself, the wilderness. [*Smile.*] But no. [*Smile broader.*] No no. [*Smile off.*] Ergo you are there. [*Pause.*] Oh no doubt you are dead, like the others, no doubt you have died, or gone away and left me, like the others, it doesn't matter, you are there. [*Pause. Eyes left.*] The bag too is there, the same as ever, I can see it. [*Pause. Eyes right. Louder.*] The bag is there, Willie, as good as ever, the one you gave me that day . . . to go to market. [*Pause. Eyes*

front.] That day. [*Pause.*] What day? [*Pause.*] I used to pray.
[*Pause.*] I say I used to pray. [*Pause.*] Yes, I must confess I did.
[*Smile.*] Not now. [*Smile broader.*] No no. [*Smile off. Pause.*]
Then . . . now . . . what difficulties here, for the mind.
[*Pause.*] To have been always what I am – and so changed
from what I was. [*Pause.*] I am the one, I say the one, then the
other. [*Pause.*] Now the one, then the other. [*Pause.*] There is
so little one can say, one says it all. [*Pause.*] All one can.
[*Pause.*] And no truth in it anywhere. [*Pause.*] My arms.
[*Pause.*] My breasts. [*Pause.*] What arms? [*Pause.*] What
breasts? [*Pause.*] Willie. [*Pause.*] What Willie? [*Sudden
vehement affirmation.*] My Willie! [*Eyes right, calling.*]
Willie! [*Pause. Louder.*] Willie! [*Pause. Eyes front.*] Ah well,
not to know, not to know for sure, great mercy, all I ask.
[*Pause.*] Ah yes . . . then . . . now . . . beechen green . . .
this . . . Charlie . . . kisses . . . this . . . all that . . . deep
trouble for the mind. [*Pause.*] But it does not trouble mine.
[*Smile.*] Not now. [*Smile broader.*] No no. [*Smile off. Long
pause. She closes eyes. Bell rings loudly. She opens eyes.
Pause.*] Eyes float up that seem to close in peace . . . to see . . .
in peace. [*Pause.*] Not mine. [*Smile.*] Not now. [*Smile
broader.*] No no. [*Smile off. Long pause.*] Willie. [*Pause.*] Do
you think the earth has lost its atmosphere, Willie? [*Pause.*]
Do you, Willie? [*Pause.*] You have no opinion? [*Pause.*] Well
that is like you, you never had any opinion about anything.
[*Pause.*] It's understandable. [*Pause.*] Most. [*Pause.*] The
earth ball. [*Pause.*] I sometimes wonder. [*Pause.*] Perhaps not
quite all. [*Pause.*] There always remains something. [*Pause.*]
Of everything. [*Pause.*] Some remains. [*Pause.*] If the mind
were to go. [*Pause.*] It won't of course. [*Pause.*] Not quite.
[*Pause.*] Not mine. [*Smile.*] Not now. [*Smile broader.*] No
no. [*Smile off. Long pause.*] It might be the eternal cold.
[*Pause.*] Everlasting perishing cold. [*Pause.*] Just chance, I
take it, happy chance. [*Pause.*] Oh yes, great mercies, great
mercies. [*Pause.*] And now? [*Long pause.*] The face.
[*Pause.*] The nose. [*She squints down.*] I can see it . . .
[*squinting down*] . . . the tip . . . the nostrils . . . breath of
life . . . that curve you so admired . . . [*pouts*] . . . a hint of
lip . . . [*pouts again*] . . . if I pout them out . . . [*sticks out

tongue] . . . the tongue of course . . . you so admired . . . if I stick it out . . . [*sticks it out again*] . . . the tip . . . [*eyes up*] . . . suspicion of brow . . . eyebrow . . . imagination possibly . . . [*eyes left*] . . . cheek . . . no . . . [*eyes right*] . . . no . . . [*distends cheeks*] . . . even if I puff them out . . . [*eyes left, distends cheeks again*] . . . no . . . no damask. [*Eyes front.*] That is all. [*Pause.*] The bag of course . . . [*eyes left*] . . . a little blurred perhaps . . . but the bag. [*Eyes front. Offhand.*] The earth of course and sky. [*Eyes right.*] The sunshade you gave me . . . that day . . . [*pause.*] . . . that day . . . the lake . . . the reeds. [*Eyes front. Pause.*] What day? [*Pause.*] What reeds? [*Long pause. Eyes close. Bell rings loudly. Eyes open. Pause. Eyes right.*] Brownie of course. [*Pause.*] You remember Brownie, Willie, I can see him. [*Pause.*] Brownie is there, Willie, beside me. [*Pause. Loud.*] Brownie is there, Willie. [*Pause. Eyes front.*] That is all. [*Pause.*] What would I do without them? [*Pause.*] What would I do without them, when words fail? [*Pause.*] Gaze before me, with compressed lips. [*Long pause while she does so.*] I cannot. [*Pause.*] Ah yes, great mercies, great mercies. [*Long pause. Low.*] Sometimes I hear sounds. [*Listening expression. Normal voice.*] But not often. [*Pause.*] They are a boon, sounds are a boon, they help me . . . through the day. [*Smile.*] The old style! [*Smile off.*] Yes, those are happy days, when there are sounds. [*Pause.*] When I hear sounds. [*Pause.*] I used to think . . . [*pause*] . . . I say I used to think they were in my head. [*Smile.*] But no. [*Smile broader.*] No no. [*Smile off.*] That was just logic. [*Pause.*] Reason. [*Pause.*] I have not lost my reason. [*Pause.*] Not yet. [*Pause.*] Not all. [*Pause.*] Some remains. [*Pause.*] Sounds. [*Pause.*] Like little . . . sunderings, little falls . . . apart. [*Pause. Low.*] It's things, Willie. [*Pause. Normal voice.*] In the bag, outside the bag. [*Pause.*] Ah yes, things have their life, that is what I always say, *things* have a life. [*Pause.*] Take my looking-glass, it doesn't need me. [*Pause.*] The bell. [*Pause.*] It hurts like a knife. [*Pause.*] A gouge. [*Pause.*] One cannot ignore it. [*Pause.*] How often . . . (*pause*) . . . I say how often I have said, Ignore it, Winnie, ignore the bell, pay no heed, just sleep and wake, sleep and wake, as you please, open and close the eyes, as you please, or in the way you find most helpful. [*Pause.*] Open and close the eyes, Winnie, open and close, always that. [*Pause.*] But no. [*Smile.*] Not now. [*Smile broader.*] No no. [*Smile off. Pause.*] What now? [*Pause.*] What now, Willie? [*Long pause.*] There is my story of course, when all else fails. [*Pause.*] A life. [*Smile.*] A long life. [*Smile off.*] Beginning in the womb, where life used to begin, Mildred has memories, she will have memories, of the womb, before she dies, the mother's womb. [*Pause.*] She is now four or five already and has recently been given a big waxen dolly. [*Pause.*] Fully clothed, complete outfit. [*Pause.*] Shoes, socks, undies, complete set, frilly frock, gloves. [*Pause.*] White mesh. [*Pause.*] A little white straw hat with a chin elastic. [*Pause.*] Pearly necklace. [*Pause.*] A little picture-book with legends in real print to go under her arm when she takes her walk. [*Pause.*] China blue eyes that open and shut. [*Pause. Narrative.*] The sun was not well up when Milly rose, descended the steep . . . [*pause*] . . . slipped on her nightgown, descended all alone the steep wooden stairs, backwards on all fours, though she had been forbidden to do so, entered the . . . [*pause*] . . . tiptoed down the silent passage, entered the nursery and began to undress Dolly. [*Pause.*] Crept under the table and began to undress Dolly. [*Pause.*] Scolding her . . . the while. [*Pause.*] Suddenly a mouse – [*Long pause.*] Gently, Winnie. [*Long pause. Calling.*] Willie! [*Pause. Louder.*] Willie! [*Pause. Mild reproach.*] I sometimes find your attitude a little strange, Willie, all this time, it is not like you to be wantonly cruel. [*Pause.*] Strange? [*Pause.*] No. [*Smile.*] Not here. [*Smile broader.*] Not now. [*Smile off.*] And yet . . . [*Suddenly anxious.*] I do hope nothing is amiss. [*Eyes right, loud.*] Is all well, dear? (*Pause. Eyes front. To herself.*] God grant he did not go in head foremost! [*Eyes right, loud.*] You're not stuck, Willie? [*Pause. Do.*] You're not jammed, Willie? [*Eyes front, distressed.*] Perhaps he is crying out for help all this time and I do not hear him! [*Pause.*] I do of course hear cries. [*Pause.*] But they are in my head surely. [*Pause.*] Is it possible that . . . [*Pause. With finality.*] No no, my head was always full of cries. [*Pause.*] Faint confused cries. [*Pause.*] They come. [*Pause.*] Then go. [*Pause.*] As on a wind. [*Pause.*] That is what I find so wonderful. [*Pause.*] They cease. [*Pause.*] Ah yes, great mercies, great mercies. [*Pause.*] The day is now well advanced. [*Smile. Smile off.*] And yet it is perhaps a little soon for my song. [*Pause.*] To sing too soon is fatal, I always find. [*Pause.*] On the other hand it is possible to leave it too late. [*Pause.*] The bell goes for sleep and one has not sung. [*Pause.*] The whole day has flown – [*smile, smile off*] – flown by, quite by, and no song of any class, kind or description. [*Pause.*] There is a problem here. [*Pause.*] One cannot sing . . . just like that, no. [*Pause.*] It bubbles up, for some unknown reason, the time is ill chosen, one chokes it back. [*Pause.*] One says, Now is the time, it is now or never, and one cannot. [*Pause.*] Simply cannot sing. [*Pause.*] Not a note. [*Pause.*] Another thing, Willie, while we are on this subject. [*Pause.*] The sadness after song. [*Pause.*] Have you run across that, Willie? [*Pause.*] In the course of your experience. [*Pause.*] No? [*Pause.*] Sadness after intimate sexual intercourse one is familiar with of course. [*Pause.*] You would concur with Aristotle there, Willie, I fancy. [*Pause.*] Yes, that one knows and is prepared to face. [*Pause.*] But after song . . . [*Pause.*] It does not last of course. [*Pause.*] That is what I find so wonderful. [*Pause.*] It wears away. [*Pause.*] What are those exquisite lines? [*Pause.*] Go forget me why should something o'er that something shadow fling . . . go forget me . . . why should sorrow . . . brightly smile . . . go forget me . . . never hear me . . . sweetly smile . . . brightly sing . . . [*Pause. With a sigh.*] One loses one's classics. [*Pause.*] Oh not all. [*Pause.*] A part. [*Pause.*] A part remains. [*Pause.*] That is what I find so wonderful, a part remains, of one's classics, to help one through the day. [*Pause.*] Oh yes, many mercies, many mercies. [*Pause.*] And now? [*Pause.*] And now, Willie? [*Long pause.*] I call to the eye of the mind . . . Mr Shower – or Cooker. [*She closes her eyes. Bell rings loudly. She opens her eyes.*

Pause.] Hand in hand, in the other hands bags. [*Pause.*]
Getting on . . . in life. [*Pause.*] No longer young, not yet
old. [*Pause.*] Standing there gaping at me. [*Pause.*] Can't
have been a bad bosom, he says, in its day. [*Pause.*] Seen
worse shoulders, he says, in my time. [*Pause.*] Does she
feel her legs? he says. [*Pause.*] Is there any life in her legs?
he says. [*Pause.*] Has she anything on underneath? he says.
[*Pause.*] Ask her, he says, I'm shy. [*Pause.*] Ask her what?
she says. [*Pause.*] Is there any life in her legs. [*Pause.*] Has
she anything on underneath. [*Pause.*] Ask her yourself, she
says. [*Pause. With sudden violence.*] Let go of me for
Christ sake and drop! [*Pause. Do.*] Drop dead! [*Smile.*]
But no. [*Smile broader.*] No no. [*Smile off.*] I watch them
recede. [*Pause.*] Hand in hand – and the bags. [*Pause.*]
Dim. [*Pause.*] Then gone. [*Pause.*] Last human kind – to
stray this way. [*Pause.*] Up to date. [*Pause.*] And now?
[*Pause. Low.*] Help. [*Pause. Do.*] Help, Willie. [*Pause.
Do.*] No? [*Long pause. Narrative.*] Suddenly a mouse . . .
[*Pause.*] Suddenly a mouse ran up her little thigh and
Mildred, dropping Dolly in her fright, began to scream –
[WINNIE *gives a sudden piercing scream*] – and screamed
and screamed – [WINNIE *screams twice*] – screamed and
screamed and screamed and screamed till all came running,
in their night attire, papa, mamma, Bibby and . . . old
Annie, to see what was the matter . . . [*pause*] . . . what on
earth could possibly be the matter. [*Pause.*] Too late.
[*Pause.*] Too late. [*Long pause. Just audible.*] Willie.
[*Pause. Normal voice.*] Ah well, not long now, Winnie,
can't be long now, until the bell for sleep. [*Pause.*] Then
you may close your eyes, then you *must* close your eyes –
and keep them closed. [*Pause.*] Why say that again?
[*Pause.*] I used to think . . . [*pause*] . . . I say I used to think
there was no difference between one fraction of a second
and the next. [*Pause.*] I used to say . . . [*pause*] . . . I say I
used to say, Winnie, you are changeless, there is never any
difference between one fraction of a second and the next.
[*Pause.*] Why bring that up again? [*Pause.*] There is so
little one can bring up, one brings up all. [*Pause.*] All one
can. [*Pause.*] My neck is hurting me. [*Pause. With sudden*

violence.] My neck is hurting me! [*Pause.*] Ah that's better.
[*With mild irritation.*] Everything within reason. [*Long
pause.*] I can do no more. [*Pause.*] Say no more. [*Pause.*]
But I must say more. [*Pause.*] Problem here. [*Pause.*] No,
something must move, in the world, I can't any more.
[*Pause.*] A zephyr. [*Pause.*] A breath. [*Pause.*] What are
those immortal lines? [*Pause.*] It might be the eternal dark.
[*Pause.*] Black night without end. [*Pause.*] Just chance, I
take it, happy chance. [*Pause.*] Oh yes, abounding mercies.
[*Long pause.*] And now? [*Pause.*] And now, Willie? [*Long
pause.*] That day. [*Pause.*] The pink fizz. [*Pause.*] The flute
glasses. [*Pause.*] The last guest gone. [*Pause.*] The last
bumper with the bodies nearly touching. [*Pause.*] The
look. [*Long pause.*] What day? [*Long pause.*] What look?
[*Long pause.*] I hear cries. [*Pause.*] Sing. [*Pause.*] Sing your
old song, Winnie.
[*Long pause. Suddenly alert expression. Eyes switch right.*
WILLIE'*s head appears to her right round corner of mound.
He is on all fours, dressed to kill – top hat, morning coat,
striped trousers, etc., white gloves in hand. Very long
bushy white Battle of Britain moustache. He halts, gazes
front, smooths moustache. He emerges completely from
behind mound, turns to his left, halts, looks up at* WINNIE.
*He advances on all fours towards centre, halts, turns head
front, gazes front, strokes moustache, straightens tie,
adjusts hat, advances a little further, halts, takes off hat
and looks up at* WINNIE. *He is now not far from centre
and within her field of vision. Unable to sustain effort of
looking up he sinks head to ground.*

WINNIE: [*Mondaine*]. Well this is an unexpected pleasure!
[*Pause.*] Reminds me of the day you came whining for my
hand. [*Pause.*] I worship you, Winnie, be mine. [*He looks
up.*] Life a mockery without Win. [*She goes off into a
giggle.*] What a get up, you do look a sight! [*Giggles.*]
Where are the flowers? [*Pause.*] That smile today. [WILLIE
sinks head.] What's that on your neck, an anthrax?
[*Pause.*] Want to watch that, Willie, before it gets a hold
on you. [*Pause.*] Where were you all this time? [*Pause.*]
What were you doing all this time? [*Pause.*] Changing?

[*Pause.*] Did you not hear me screaming for you? [*Pause.*] Did you get stuck in your hole? [*Pause. He looks up.*] That's right, Willie, look at me. [*Pause.*] Feast your old eyes, Willie. [*Pause.*] Does anything remain? [*Pause.*] Any remains? [*Pause.*] No? [*Pause.*] I haven't been able to look after it, you know. [*He sinks his head.*] You are still recognizable, in a way. [*Pause.*] Are you thinking of coming to live this side now . . . for a bit maybe? [*Pause.*] No? [*Pause.*] Just a brief call? [*Pause.*] Have you gone deaf, Willie? [*Pause.*] Dumb? [*Pause.*] Oh I know you were never one to talk, I worship you Winnie be mine and then nothing from that day forth only titbits from *Reynolds' News.* [*Eyes front. Pause.*] Ah well, what matter, that's what I always say, it will have been a happy day, after all, another happy day. [*Pause.*] Not long now, Winnie. [*Pause.*] I hear cries. [*Pause.*] Do you ever hear cries, Willie? [*Pause.*] No? [*Eyes back on* WILLIE.] Willie. [*Pause.*] Look at me again, Willie. [*Pause.*] Once more, Willie. [*He looks up. Happily.*] Ah! [*Pause. Shocked.*] What ails you, Willie, I never saw such an expression! [*Pause.*] Put on your hat, dear, it's the sun, don't stand on ceremony, I won't mind. [*He drops hat and gloves and starts to crawl up mound towards her. Gleeful.*] Oh I say, this is terrific! [*He halts, clinging to mound with one hand, reaching up with the other.*] Come on, dear, put a bit of jizz into it, I'll cheer you on. [*Pause.*] Is it me you're after, Willie . . . or is it something else? [*Pause.*] Do you want to touch my face . . . again? [*Pause.*] Is it a kiss you're after, Willie . . . or is it something else? [*Pause.*] There was a time when I could have given you a hand. [*Pause.*] And then a time before that again when I did give you a hand. [*Pause.*] You were always in dire need of a hand, Willie. [*He slithers back to foot of mound and lies with face to ground.*] Brrum! [*Pause. He rises to hands and knees, raises his face towards her.*] Have another go, Willie, I'll cheer you on. [*Pause.*] Don't look at me like that! [*Pause. Vehement.*] Don't look at me like that! [*Pause. Low.*] Have you gone off your head, Willie? [*Pause. Do.*] Out of your poor old wits, Willie? [*Pause.*]

WILLIE: [*Just audible.*] Win.

[*Pause.* WINNIE's *eyes front. Happy expression appears, grows.*]

WINNIE: Win! [*Pause.*] Oh this *is* a happy day, this will have been another happy day! [*Pause.*] After all. [*Pause.*] So far. [*Pause. She hums tentatively beginning of song, then sings softly, musical-box tune.*]

> Though I say not
> What I may not
> Let you hear,
> Yet the swaying
> Dance is saying,
> Love me dear!
> Every touch of fingers
> Tells me what I know,
> Says for you,
> It's true, it's true,
> You love me so!

(*Pause. Happy expression off. She closes her eyes. Bell rings loudly. She opens her eyes. She smiles, gazing front. She turns her eyes, smiling, to* WILLIE, *still on his hands and knees looking up at her. Smile off. They look at each other. Long pause.*]

CURTAIN